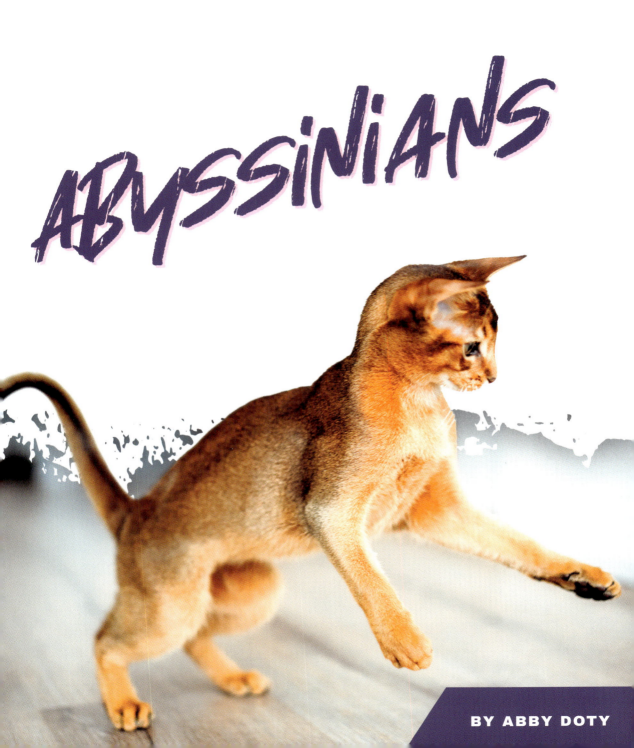

CAT BREEDS

ABYSSINIANS

BY ABBY DOTY

WWW.APEXEDITIONS.COM

Copyright © 2025 by Apex Editions, Mendota Heights, MN 55120. All rights reserved. No part of this book may be reproduced or utilized in any form or by any means without written permission from the publisher.

Apex is distributed by North Star Editions:
sales@northstareditions.com | 888-417-0195

Produced for Apex by Red Line Editorial.

Photographs ©: Shutterstock Images, cover, 1, 4–5, 6, 7, 8, 10–11, 12–13, 14–15, 16–17, 18, 19, 20–21, 22–23, 24–25, 26, 29

Library of Congress Control Number: 2024940140

ISBN
979-8-89250-305-1 (hardcover)
979-8-89250-343-3 (paperback)
979-8-89250-418-8 (ebook pdf)
979-8-89250-381-5 (hosted ebook)

Printed in the United States of America
Mankato, MN
012025

NOTE TO PARENTS AND EDUCATORS
Apex books are designed to build literacy skills in striving readers. Exciting, high-interest content attracts and holds readers' attention. The text is carefully leveled to allow students to achieve success quickly. Additional features, such as bolded glossary words for difficult terms, help build comprehension.

TABLE OF CONTENTS

CHAPTER 1
ON THE MOVE 4

CHAPTER 2
BREED HISTORY 10

CHAPTER 3
ACTIVE ABYSSINIANS 16

CHAPTER 4
CAT CARE 22

COMPREHENSION QUESTIONS • 28
GLOSSARY • 30
TO LEARN MORE • 31
ABOUT THE AUTHOR • 31
INDEX • 32

CHAPTER 1

ON THE MOVE

A young Abyssinian cat runs through the house. She climbs up her cat tree. She plops down on the top platform.

Many Abyssinians love to climb. Cat trees give them high places to perch.

Abyssinians often jump high onto shelves.

A few minutes later, the Abyssinian jumps to a nearby shelf. Then, her owner walks into the room. The cat runs to him and **chirps** happily.

FAST FACT

Abyssinians don't meow often. But they sometimes make soft sounds.

Abyssinians may follow their owners around the house.

The owner takes out a feather toy and **dangles** it above the Abyssinian. The cat pounces at the toy. She leaps high into the air and grabs it.

TONS OF TRICKS

Abyssinians are one of the smartest cat **breeds**. Many owners teach them tricks. Some Abyssinians learn to play fetch. The cats can also learn to sit or shake hands.

◄ Cats are natural hunters. Many like to chase and catch toys.

CHAPTER 2

BREED HISTORY

Abyssinians are one of the oldest cat breeds. People in England have owned them since the late 1800s. But the breed's **origins** are uncertain.

Many people think Abyssinians look like cat artwork from Ancient Egypt.

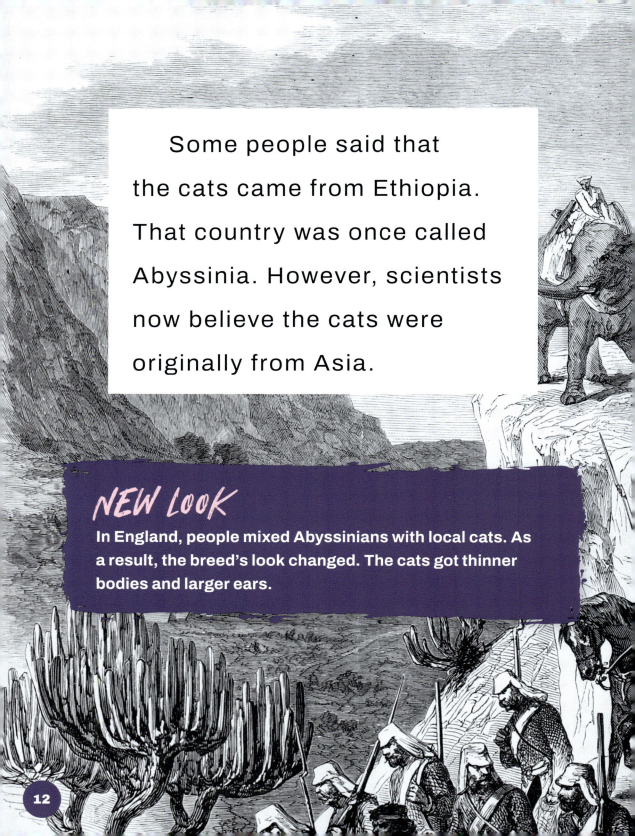

Some people said that the cats came from Ethiopia. That country was once called Abyssinia. However, scientists now believe the cats were originally from Asia.

NEW LOOK

In England, people mixed Abyssinians with local cats. As a result, the breed's look changed. The cats got thinner bodies and larger ears.

British soldiers fought in Ethiopia during the 1800s. Some people claimed they brought cats back home.

In the early 1900s, Abyssinians began to spread from England to other countries. Today, they are one of the world's most **popular** cat breeds.

FAST FACT

During World War II (1939–1945), Abyssinians in Europe nearly died out. But they survived in North America.

In 1929, Abyssinians became an official breed in England.

CHAPTER 3

ACTIVE ABYSSINIANS

Abyssinians have strong **muscles**. Their bodies are long and **lean**. The cats can weigh up to 12 pounds (5 kg).

Abyssinians are active cats. They use their muscles to run and jump.

An Abyssinian's almond-shaped eyes can be green, gold, or hazel.

Abyssinians have large ears and pointed faces. The cats have short fur. The fur has a **ticked** pattern. Each hair has strips of light and dark colors.

COAT COLORS

Abyssinians come in a few colors. Many have ruddy coats. These cats have dark-orange fur and brown or black ticking. Fur can also be reddish, gray, or light brown.

Fawn-coated Abyssinians are rare. These cats have light-brown fur.

Abyssinians are curious cats. They like to **explore**, climb, and play. The cats are also social. They like to spend time with their owners.

FAST FACT

Abyssinians sometimes sit on their owners' shoulders.

CHAPTER 4

CAT CARE

Once a week, owners should brush their Abyssinians' fur. Owners should also brush the cats' teeth several times a week.

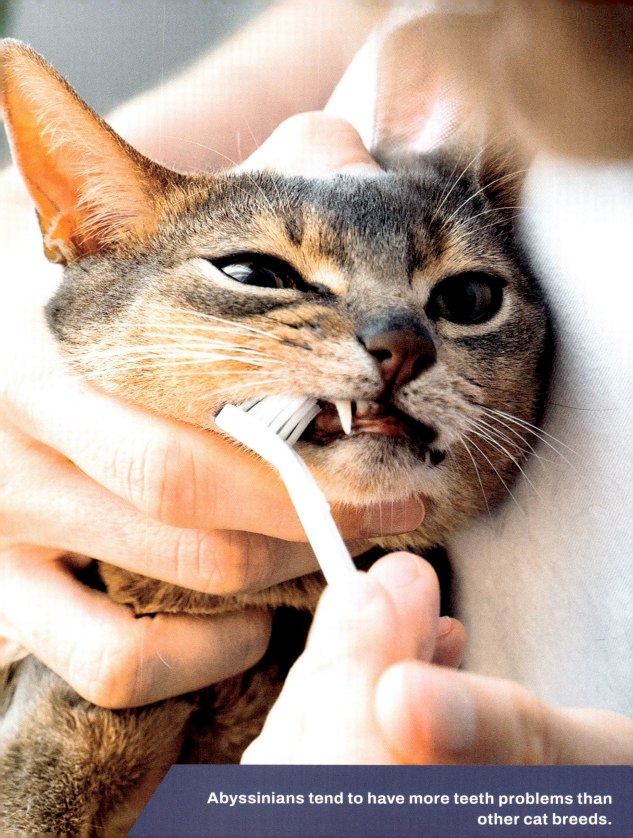

Abyssinians tend to have more teeth problems than other cat breeds.

Abyssinians are energetic. They need at least 30 minutes of exercise each day. They may get bored if left alone for too long. Cat furniture and toys can help them stay busy.

MIND GAMES

Abyssinians need exercise for their minds. Food puzzles can help. Owners give the puzzles to cats. Food is stored inside. Cats get the food out with their paws and tongues.

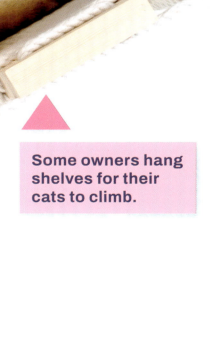

Some owners hang shelves for their cats to climb.

25

Abyssinians can be good pets for families. They do best with older children and adults. They also get along with other animals.

FAST FACT
Owning two cats can be helpful. The cats can play together while their owners are away.

◀ **Abyssinians move around a lot. The cats usually do not like to be held by owners.**

COMPREHENSION QUESTIONS

Write your answers on a separate piece of paper.

1. Write a few sentences explaining the main ideas of Chapter 3.

2. Would you like to have a pet Abyssinian? Why or why not?

3. How often should owners brush their Abyssinians' fur?
   - A. daily
   - B. weekly
   - C. monthly

4. What is the Abyssinian breed named after?
   - A. the people who first brought the cats to North America
   - B. the place some people said the cats were from
   - C. the color of the cats' fur

5. What does **pounces** mean in this book?

*The cat **pounces** at the toy. She leaps high into the air and grabs it.*

    A. yells
    B. sits
    C. jumps

6. What does **energetic** mean in this book?

*Abyssinians are **energetic**. They need at least 30 minutes of exercise each day.*

    A. active
    B. lazy
    C. hungry

Answer key on page 32.

GLOSSARY

breeds
Specific types of cats that have their own looks and abilities.

chirps
Makes a short, high-pitched sound.

dangles
Hangs or waves above the ground.

explore
To search or move through an area.

lean
Thin and fit.

muscles
Parts of the body that help with strength and movement.

origins
The early parts of something's history.

popular
Liked by or known to many people.

ticked
Having two or more bands of color on a single hair.

BOOKS

Clausen-Grace, Nicki. *Abyssinians*. Mankato, MN: Black Rabbit Books, 2020.

Pearson, Marie. *Cat Behavior*. Minneapolis: Abdo Publishing, 2024.

Watts, Robyn. *Clever Cats!* Sandgate, Queensland, Australia: Knowledge Books, 2024.

ONLINE RESOURCES

Visit **www.apexeditions.com** to find links and resources related to this title.

ABOUT THE AUTHOR

Abby Doty is a writer, editor, and booklover from Minnesota.

INDEX

A
Abyssinia, 12
Asia, 12

B
breeds, 9, 10, 14

C
children, 27
chirping, 6
colors, 18–19

E
England, 10, 12, 14
Ethiopia, 12
Europe, 14
exercise, 24–25

F
fur, 18–19, 22

M
muscles, 16

N
North America, 14

O
origins, 10

P
puzzles, 25

T
teeth, 22
ticked, 18

W
World War II, 14

ANSWER KEY:
1. Answers will vary; 2. Answers will vary; 3. B; 4. B; 5. C; 6. A